The Trotskyist Opposition Before and Now
Joseph Stalin

The Trotskyist Opposition Before and Now

Joseph Stalin

Published 2022 Wheeling, WVa

ISBN 978-1-716-01663-9

Contents

Some Minor Questions

Speech Delivered at a Meeting of the Joint Plenum of the Central Committee and the Central Control Commission of the C.P.S.U.(B.), October 23, 1927

Comrades, I have not much time; I shall therefore deal with separate questions. First of all about the personal factor. You have heard here how assiduously the oppositionists hurl abuse at Stalin, abuse him with all their might. That does not surprise me, comrades. The reason why the main attacks were directed against Stalin is because Stalin knows all the opposition's tricks better, perhaps, than some of our comrades do, and it is not so easy, I dare say, to fool him. So they strike their blows primarily at Stalin. Well, let them hurl abuse to their heart's content.

And what is Stalin? Stalin is only a minor figure. Take Lenin. Who does not know that at the time of the August bloc the opposition, headed by Trotsky, waged an even more scurrilous campaign of slander against Lenin? Listen to Trotsky, for example:

"The wretched squabbling systematically provoked by Lenin, that old hand at the game, that professional exploiter of all that is backward in the Russian labour movement, seems like a senseless obsession" (see "Trotsky's Letter to Chkheidze," April 1913).

Note the language, comrades! Note the language! It is Trotsky writing. And writing about Lenin.

Is it surprising, then, that Trotsky, who wrote in such an ill-mannered way about the great Lenin, whose shoe-laces he was not worthy of tying, should now hurl abuse at one of Lenin's numerous pupils—Comrade Stalin?

More than that. I think the opposition does me honour by

"

venting all its hatred against Stalin. That is as it should be. I think it would be strange and offensive if the opposition, which is trying to wreck the Party, were to praise Stalin, who is defending the fundamentals of the Leninist Party principle.

Now about Lenin's "will." The oppositionists shouted here—you heard them—that the Central Committee of the Party "concealed" Lenin's "will." We have discussed this question several times at the plenum of the Central Committee and Central Control Commission, you know that. (A voice: "Scores of times.") It has been proved and proved again that nobody has concealed anything, that Lenin's "will" was addressed to the Thirteenth Party Congress, that this "will" was read out at the congress (*Voices:* "That's right!"), that the congress *unanimously* decided not to publish it because, among other things, Lenin himself did not want it to be published and did not ask that it should be published. The opposition knows all this just as well as we do. Nevertheless, it has the audacity to declare that the Central Committee is "concealing" the "will."

The question of Lenin's "will" was brought up, if I am not mistaken, as far back as 1924. There is a certain Eastman, a former American Communist who was later expelled from the Party. This gentleman, who mixed with the Trotskyists in Moscow, picked up some rumours and gossip about Lenin's "will," went abroad and published a book entitled *After Lenin's Death,* in which he did his best to blacken the Party, the Central Committee and the Soviet regime, and the gist of which was that the Central Committee of our Party was "concealing" Lenin's "will." In view of the fact that this Eastman had at one time been connected with Trotsky, we, the members of the Political Bureau, called upon Trotsky to dissociate himself from Eastman who, clutching at Trotsky and referring to the opposition, had made Trotsky responsible for the slanderous statements against our Party about the "will." Since the question was so obvious, Trotsky did, indeed, publicly dissociate himself from Eastman in a statement he made in the press. It was published in September 1925 in *Bolshevik,* No. 16.

Permit me to read the passage in Trotsky's article in which he deals with the question whether the Party and its Central Committee was concealing Lenin's "will" or not. I quote Trotsky's article:

"In several parts of his book Eastman says that the Central Committee 'concealed' from the Party a number of exceptionally important documents written by Lenin in the last period of his life (it is a matter of letters on the national question, the so-called 'will,' and others); *there can be no other name for this than slander against the Central Committee of our Party.* From what Eastman says it may be inferred that Vladimir Ilyich intended those letters, which bore the character of advice on internal organisation, for the press. In point of fact, that is absolutely untrue. During his illness Vladimir Ilyich often sent proposals, letters, and so forth, to the Party's leading institutions and to its congress. It goes without saying that all those letters and proposals were always delivered to those for whom they were intended, were brought to the knowledge of the delegates at the Twelfth and Thirteenth Congresses, and always, of course, exercised due influence upon the Party's decisions; and if not all of those letters were published, it was because the author did not intend them for the press. Vladimir Ilyich did not leave any 'will,' and the very character of his attitude towards the Party, as well as the character of the Party itself, precluded the possibility of such a 'will.' What is usually referred to as a 'will' in the emigre and foreign bourgeois and Menshevik press (in a manner garbled beyond recognition) is one of Vladimir Ilyich's letters containing advice on organisational matters. The Thirteenth Congress of the Party paid the closest attention to that letter, as to all of the others, and drew from it conclusions appropriate to the conditions and circumstances of the time. *All talk about concealing or violating a 'will' is a malicious invention and is entirely directed against Vladimir Ilyich's real will,* and against the interests of the Party he created" (see Trotsky's article "Concerning Eastman's Book *After Lenin's Death,"* *Bolshevik,* No. 16, September 1, 1925, p. 68).

Clear, one would think. That was written by none other than Trotsky. On what grounds, then, are Trotsky, Zinoviev and Kamenev now spinning a yarn about the Party and its Central Committee "concealing" Lenin's "will"? It is "permissible" to spin yarns, but one should know where to stop.

It is said that in that "will" Comrade Lenin suggested to the congress that in view of Stalin's "rudeness" it should consider the question of putting another comrade in Stalin's place as General Secretary. That is quite true. Yes, comrades, I am rude to those who grossly and perfidiously wreck and split the Party. I have never concealed this and do not conceal it now. Perhaps some mildness is needed in the treatment of splitters, but I am a bad hand at that. At the very first meeting of the plenum of the Central Committee after the Thirteenth Congress I asked the plenum of the Central Committee to release me from my duties as General Secretary. The congress itself discussed this question. It was discussed by each delegation separately, and all the delegations unanimously, including Trotsky, Kamenev and Zinoviev, *obliged* Stalin to remain at his post.

What could I do? Desert my post? That is not in my nature; I have never deserted any post, and I have no right to do so, for that would be desertion. As I have already said before, I am not a free agent, and when the Party imposes an obligation upon me, I must obey.

A year later I again put in a request to the plenum to release me, but I was again obliged to remain at my post.

What else could I do?

As regards publishing the "will," the congress decided not to publish it, since it was addressed to the congress and was not intended for publication.

We have the decision of a plenum of the Central Committee and Central Control Commission in 1926 to ask the Fifteenth Congress for permission to publish this document. We have the decision of the same plenum of the Central Committee and Central Control Commission to publish other letters of Lenin's, in which he pointed out the mistakes of Kamenev and Zinoviev just before the October uprising and demanded their expulsion from the Party.

Obviously, talk about the Party concealing these documents is infamous slander. Among these documents are letters from Lenin urging the necessity of expelling Zinoviev and Kamenev from the Party. The Bolshevik Party, the Central Committee of the Bolshevik

Party, have never feared the truth. The strength of the Bolshevik Party lies precisely in the fact that it does not fear the truth and looks the truth straight in the face.

The opposition is trying to use Lenin's "will" as a trump card; but it is enough to read this "will" to see that it is not a trump card for them at all. On the contrary, Lenin's "will" is fatal to the present leaders of the opposition.

Indeed, it is a fact that in his "will" Lenin accuses Trotsky of being guilty of "non-Bolshevism" and, as regards the mistake Kamenev and Zinoviev made during October, he says that that mistake was not "accidental." What does that mean? It means that Trotsky, who suffers from "non-Bolshevism," and Kamenev and Zi-noviev, whose mistakes are not "accidental" and can and certainly will be repeated, cannot be *politically* trusted.

It is characteristic that there is not a word, not a hint in the "will" about Stalin having made mistakes. It refers only to Stalin's rudeness. But rudeness is not and cannot be counted as a defect in Stalin's *political* line or position.

Here is the relevant passage in the "will":

"I shall not go on to characterise the personal qualities of the other members of the Central Committee. I shall merely remind you that the October episode with Zinoviev and Kamenev was, of course, not accidental, but that they can be blamed for it personally as little as Trotsky can be blamed for his non-Bolshevism."

Clear, one would think.

The Opposition's "Platform"

Next question. Why did not the Central Committee publish the opposition's "platform"? Zinoviev and Trotsky say that it was because the Central Committee and the Party "fear" the truth. Is that true? Of course not. More than that. It is absurd to say that the Party or the Central Committee fear the truth. We have the verbatim reports of the plenums of the Central Committee and Central Control Commission. Those reports have been printed in several thousand copies and distributed among the members of the Party. They contain the speeches of the oppositionists as well as of the representatives of the Party line. They are being read by tens and hundreds of thousands of Party members. (*Voices:* "That's true!") If we feared the truth we would not have circulated those documents. The good thing about those documents is precisely that they enable the members of the Party to compare the Central Committee's position with the views of the opposition and to make their decision. Is that fear of the truth?

In October 1926, the leaders of the opposition strutted about and asserted, as they are asserting now, that the Central Committee feared the truth, that it was hiding their "platform," concealing it from the Party, and so forth. That is why they went snooping among the Party units in Moscow (recall the Aviapribor Factory), in Leningrad (recall the Putilov Works), and other places. Well, what happened? The communist workers gave our oppositionists a good drubbing, such a drubbing indeed that the leaders of the opposition were compelled to flee from the battlefield. Why did they not at that time dare to go farther, to all the Party units, to ascertain which of us fears the truth—the opposition or the Central Committee? It was because they got cold feet, being frightened by the real (and not imaginary) truth.

And now? Speaking honestly, is not a discussion going on now in the Party units? Point to at least one unit, containing at least one oppositionist and where at least one meeting has been held during the past three or four months, in which representatives of the opposition have not spoken, in which there has been no discussion. Is it not a fact that during the past three or four months the opposition has been coming forward whenever it could in the Party units with its counter-resolutions? (*Voices:* "Quite true!") Why, then, do not Trotsky and Zinoviev try to go to the Party units and expound their views?

A characteristic fact. In August this year, after the plenum of the Central Committee and Central Control Commission, Trotsky and Zinoviev sent in a statement that they wanted to speak at a meeting of the Moscow active if the Central Committee had no objection. To this the Central Committee replied (and the reply was circulated among the local organisations) that it had no objection to Trotsky and Zinoviev speaking at such a meeting, provided, however, that they, as members of the Central Committee, did not speak against the decisions of the Central Committee. What happened? They dropped their request. (*General laughter.*)

Yes, comrades, somebody among us does fear the truth, but it is not the Central Committee, and still less the Party; it is the leaders of our opposition.

That being the case, why did not the Central Committee publish the opposition's "platform"?

Firstly, because the Central Committee did not want and had no right to legalise Trotsky's faction, or any factional group. In the Tenth Congress resolution "On Unity," Lenin said that the existence of a "platform" is one of the principal signs of factionalism. In spite of that, the opposition drew up a "platform" and demanded that it be published, thereby violating the decision of the Tenth Congress. Supposing the Central Committee had published the opposition's "platform," what would it have meant? It would have meant that the Central Committee was willing to participate in the opposition's factional efforts to violate the decisions of the Tenth Congress. Could the Central Committee and the Central Control Commission agree to do that? Obviously, no self-respecting Central Committee could take that factional step. (*Voices:* "Quite true!")

Further. In this same Tenth Congress resolution "On Unity," written by Lenin, it is said: "The congress orders the immediate *dissolution* of all groups without exception that have been formed on the basis of one platform or another," that "non-observance of this decision of the congress shall involve certain and immediate expulsion from the Party." The directive is clear and definite. Supposing the Central Committee and the Central Control Commission had published the opposition's "platform," could that have been called the dissolution of all groups without exception formed on one "platform" or another? Obviously not. On the contrary, it would have meant that the Central Committee and the Central Control Commission themselves were intending not to dissolve, but to help to organise groups and factions on the basis of the opposition's "platform." Could the Central Committee and the Central Control Commission take that step towards splitting the Party? Obviously, they could not.

Finally, the opposition's "platform" contains slanders against the Party which, if published, would do the Party and our state irreparable harm.

In fact, it is stated in the opposition's "platform" that our Party is willing to abolish the monopoly of foreign trade and make payment on all debts, hence, also on the war debts. Everybody knows that this is a disgusting slander against our Party, against our working class, against our state. Supposing we had published the "platform" containing this slander against the Party and the state, what would have happened? The only result would have been that the international bourgeoisie would have begun to exert greater pressure upon us, it would have demanded concessions to which we could not agree at all (for example, the abolition of the monopoly of foreign trade, payments on the war debts, and so forth) and would have threatened us with war.

When members of the Central Committee like Trotsky and Zinoviev supply false reports about our Party to the imperialists of all countries, assuring them that we are ready to make the utmost concessions, including the abolition of the monopoly of foreign trade, it can have only one meaning: Messieurs the bourgeois, press harder on the Bolshevik Party, threaten to go to war against them; the Bolsheviks will agree to every concession if you press hard enough.

False reports about our Party lodged with Messieurs the

imperialists by Zinoviev and Trotsky in order to aggravate our difficulties in the sphere of foreign policy—that is what the opposition's "platform" amounts to.

Whom does this harm? Obviously, it harms the proletariat of the U.S.S.R., the Communist Party of the U.S.S.R., our whole state.

Whom does it benefit? It benefits the imperialists of all countries.

Now I ask you: could the Central Committee agree to publish such filth in our press? Obviously, it could not.

Such are the considerations that compelled the Central Committee to refuse to publish the opposition's "platform."

Lenin on Discussions and Oppositions in General

The next question. Zinoviev vehemently tried to prove that Lenin was in favour of discussion always and at all times. He referred to the discussion of various platforms that took place before the Tenth Congress and at the congress itself, but he "forgot" to mention that Lenin regarded the discussion that took place before the Tenth Congress as a mistake. He "forgot" to say that the Tenth Congress resolution "On Party Unity," which was written by Lenin and was a *directive* for the development of our Party, ordered not the discussion of "platforms," but the dissolution of all groups whatsoever formed on the basis of one "platform" or another. He "forgot" that at the Tenth Congress Lenin spoke in favour of the "prohibition" in future of all oppositions in the Party. He "forgot" to say that Lenin regarded the conversion of our Party into a "debating society" as absolutely impermissible.

Here, for example, is Lenin's appraisal of the discussion that took place prior to the Tenth Congress:

"I have already had occasion to speak about this today and, of course, I could only cautiously observe that there can hardly be many among you who do not regard this discussion as an excessive luxury. I cannot refrain from adding that, speaking for myself, I think that this luxury was indeed absolutely impermissible, and that in permitting such a discussion we undoubtedly made a mistake" (see Minutes of the Tenth Congress, p. 16).

And here is what Lenin said at the Tenth Congress about any possible opposition after the Tenth Congress:

"Consolidation of the Party, prohibition of an opposition in the Party —such is the political conclusion to be drawn from the present situation. . . ." "We do not want an opposition now, comrades. And I

16

think that the Party congress will have to draw this conclusion, to draw the conclusion that we must now put an end to the opposition, finish with it, we have had enough of oppositions now!" (*Ibid.,* pp. 61 and 63.)

That is how Lenin regarded the question of discussion and of opposition in general.

The Opposition and the "Third Force"

The next question. What was the need for Comrade Menzhinsky's statement about the whiteguards with whom some of the "workers" at the Trotskyists' illegal, anti-Party printing press are connected?

Firstly, in order to dispel the lie and slander that the opposition is spreading in connection with this question in its anti-Party sheets. The opposition assures everyone that the report about whiteguards who are con nected in one way or another with allies of the opposition like Shcherbakov, Tverskoy, and others, is fiction, an invention, put into circulation for the purpose of discrediting the opposition. Comrade Menzhinsky's statement, with the depositions made by the people under arrest, leaves no doubt whatever that a section of the "workers" at the Trotskyists' illegal, anti-Party printing press are connected, indubitably connected, with white-guard counter-revolutionary elements. Let the opposition try to refute those facts and documents.

Secondly, in order to expose the lies now being spread by Maslow's organ in Berlin (Die *Fahne des Kommu-nismus,* that is, *The Banner of Communism*). We have just received the last issue of this filthy rag, published by this renegade Maslow, who is occupied in slandering the U.S.S.R. and betraying state secrets of the U.S.S.R. to the bourgeoisie. This organ of the press prints for public information, in a garbled form, of course, the depositions made by the arrested whiteguards and their allies at the illegal, anti-Party printing press. (*Voices:* "Scandalous!") Where could Maslow get this information from? This information is secret, for not all the members of the whiteguard band that is involved in the business of organising a conspiracy on the lines of the Pilsudski conspiracy have as yet been traced and arrested. This information was made known in the Central Control Commission to Trotsky, Zinoviev, Smilga and other members of the opposition. They were forbidden to make a copy of those depositions for the time being. But evidently, they did make a copy and hastened to send it to Maslow. But what does sending that information to Maslow for publication mean? It means warning the whiteguards who have not yet been traced and arrested, warning them that the Bolsheviks intend to arrest them.

Is it proper, is it permissible for Communists to do a thing like that? Obviously not.

The article in Maslow's organ bears a piquant heading: "Stalin Is Splitting the C.P.S.U.(B.). A Whiteguard Conspiracy. A Letter from the U.S.S.R." (*Voices:* "Scoundrels!") Could we, after all this, after Maslow, with the aid of Trotsky and Zinoviev, had printed for public information garbled depositions of people under arrest, could we, after all this, refrain from making a report to the plenum of the Central Committee and Central Control Commission and from contrasting the lying stories with the actual facts and the actual depositions?

That is why the Central Committee and the Central Control Commission considered it necessary to ask Comrade Menzhinsky to make a statement about the facts.

What follows from these depositions, from Comrade Menzhinsky's statement? Have we ever accused or are we now accusing the opposition of organising a military conspiracy? Of course, not. Have we ever accused or are we now accusing the opposition of taking part in this conspiracy? Of course, not. (*Muralov:* "You did make the accusation at the last plenum.") That is not true, Muralov. We have two statements by the Central Committee and the Central Control Commission about the illegal, anti-Party printing press and about the non-Party intellectuals connected with that printing press. You will not find a single sentence, not a single word, in those documents to show that we are accusing the opposition of participating in a military conspiracy. In those documents the Central Committee and the Central Control Commission merely assert that, when organising its illegal printing press, the opposition got into contact with bourgeois intellectuals, and that some of these intellectuals were, in their turn, found to be in contact with whiteguards who were hatching a military conspiracy. I would ask Muralov to point out the relevant passage in the documents published by the Political Bureau of the Central Committee and the Presidium of the Central Control Commission in connection with this question. Muralov cannot point out such a passage because it does not exist.

That being the case, what are the charges we have made and still make against the opposition?

Firstly, that the opposition, in pursuing a splitting policy, organised an anti-Party, illegal printing press.

Secondly, that the opposition, for the purpose of organising this printing press, entered into a bloc with bourgeois intellectuals, part of whom turned out to be in direct contact with counter-revolutionary conspirators.

Thirdly, that, by enlisting the services of bourgeois intellectuals and conspiring with them against the Party, the opposition, independently of its will or desire, found itself encircled by the so-called "third force."

The opposition proved to have much more confidence in those bourgeois intellectuals than in its own Party. Otherwise it would not have demanded the release of "all those arrested" in connection with the illegal printing press, including Shcherbakov, Tverskoy, Bolshakov and others, who were found to be in contact with counterrevolutionary elements.

The opposition wanted to have an anti-Party, illegal printing press; for that purpose it had recourse to the aid of bourgeois intellectuals, but some of those intellectuals proved to be in contact with downright counterrevolutionaries—such is the chain that resulted, comrades. Independently of the opposition's will or desire, anti-Soviet elements flocked round it and strove to utilise its splitting activities for their own ends.

, what Lenin predicted as far back as the Tenth Congress of our Party (see the Tenth Congress resolution "On Party Unity"), where he said that the "third force," that is the bourgeoisie, would certainly try to hitch on to the conflict within our Party in order to utilise the opposition's activities for its own class ends, has come true.

It is said that counter-revolutionary elements sometimes penetrate our Soviet bodies also, at the fronts for example without having any connection with the opposition. That is true. In such cases, however, the Soviet authorities arrest those elements and shoot them. But what did the opposition do? It demanded the release of the bourgeois intellectuals who were arrested in connection with the illegal printing press and were found to be in contact with counter-revolutionary elements. That is the trouble, comrades. That is what the opposition's splitting activities lead to. Instead of thinking of all these dangers, instead of thinking of the pit that is yawning in front of them, our oppositionists heap slander on the Party and try with all their might to disorganise, to split our Party.

There is talk about a former Wrangel officer who is helping the OGPU to unmask counter-revolutionary organisations. The opposition leaps and dances and makes a great fuss about the fact that the former Wrangel officer to whom the opposition's allies, all these Shcherbakovs and Tverskoys, applied for assistance, proved to be an agent of the OGPU. But is there anything wrong in this former Wrangel officer helping the Soviet authorities to unmask counter-revolutionary conspiracies? Who can deny the right of the Soviet authorities to win former officers to their side in order to employ them for the purpose of unmasking counter-revolutionary organisations?

Shcherbakov and Tverskoy addressed themselves to this former Wrangel officer not because he was an agent of the OGPU, but because he was a former Wrangel officer, and they did so in order to employ him against the Party and *against* the Soviet Government. That is the point, and that is the misfortune of our opposition. And when, following up these clues, the OGPU quite unexpectedly came across the Trotskyists' illegal, anti-Party printing press, it found that, while arranging a bloc with the opposition, Messieurs the Shcherbakovs, Tverskoys and Bolshakovs were already in a bloc with counter-revolutionaries, with former Kolchak officers like Kostrov and Novikov, as Comrade Menzhinsky reported to you today.

That is the point, comrades, and that is the trouble with our opposition.

The opposition's splitting activities lead it to linking up with bourgeois intellectuals, and the link with bourgeois intellectuals makes it easy for all sorts of counter-revolutionary elements to envelop it—that is the bitter truth.

How the Opposition is "Preparing" for the Congress

The next question: about the preparations for the congress. Zinoviev and Trotsky vehemently asserted here that we are preparing for the congress by means of repression. It is strange that they see nothing but "repression." But what about the decision to open a discussion taken by a plenum of the Central Committee and Central Control Commission more than a month before the congress—is that in your opinion preparation for the congress, or is it not? And what about the discussion in the Party units and other Party organisations that has been going on incessantly for three or four months already? And the discussion of the verbatim reports and decisions of the plenum that has been going on for the past six months, particularly the past three or four months, on all questions concerning home and foreign policy? What else can all this be called if not stimulating the activity of the Party membership drawing it into the discussion of the major questions of our policy, preparing the Party membership for the congress?

Who is to blame if, in all this, the Party organisations do not support the opposition? Obviously, the opposition is to blame, for its line is one of utter bankruptcy, its policy is that of a bloc with all the anti-Party elements, including the renegades Maslow and Souvarine, against the Party and the Comintern.

Evidently, Zinoviev and Trotsky think that preparations for the congress ought to be made by organising illegal, anti-Party printing presses, by organising illegal, anti-Party meetings, by supplying false reports about our Party to the imperialists of all countries, by disorganising and splitting our Party. You will agree that this is a rather strange idea of what preparations for the Party congress mean. And when the Party takes resolute measures, including expulsion, against the dis-organisers and splitters, the opposition raises a howl about repression.

Yes, the Party resorts and will resort to repression against disorganisers and splitters, for the Party must not be split under any circumstances, either before the congress or during the congress. It would be suicidal for the Party to allow out-and-out splitters, the allies of all sorts of Shcherbakovs, to wreck the Party just because only a month remains before the congress.

Comrade Lenin saw things in a different light. You know that in 1921 Lenin proposed that Shlyapnikov be expelled from the Central Committee and from the Party not for organising an anti-Party printing press, and not for allying himself with bourgeois intellectuals, but merely because, at a meeting of a Party unit, Shlyapnikov dared to criticise the decisions of the Supreme Council of National Economy. If you compare this attitude of Lenin's with what the Party is now doing to the opposition, you will realise what licence we have allowed the disorganisers and splitters.

You surely must know that in 1917, just before the October uprising, Lenin several times proposed that Kamenev and Zinoviev be expelled from the Party merely because they had criticised unpublished Party decisions in the semi-socialist, in the semi-bourgeois newspaper *Novaya* Zhinn. But how many secret decisions of the Central Committee and the Central Control Commission are now being published by our opposition in the columns of Maslow's newspaper in Berlin, which is a bourgeois, anti-Soviet, counter-revolutionary newspaper! Yet we tolerate all this, tolerate it without end, and thereby give the splitters in the opposition the opportunity to wreck our Party. Such is the disgrace to which the opposition has brought us! But we cannot tolerate it forever, comrades. (*Voices:* "Quite right!" *Applause.*)

It is said that disorganisers who have been expelled from the Party and conduct anti-Soviet activities are being arrested. Yes, we arrest them, and we shall do so in future if they do not stop undermining the Party and the Soviet regime. (*Voices:* "Quite right! Quite right!")

It is said that such things are unprecedented in the history of our Party. That is not true. What about the Myasnikov group? What about the "Workers' Truth" group? Who does not know that the members of those groups were arrested with the full consent of Zinoviev, Trotsky and Kamenev? Why was it permissible three or four years ago to arrest disorganisers who had been expelled from the Party, but is impermissible now, when some of the former members of the Trotskyist opposition go to the length of directly linking up with counterrevolutionaries?

You heard Comrade Menzhinsky's statement. In that statement it is said that a certain Stepanov (an army-man), a member of the Party, a supporter of the opposition, is in direct contact with counter-revolutionaries, with Novikov, Kostrov and others, which Stepanov himself does not deny in his depositions. What do you want us to do with this fellow, who is in the opposition to this day? Kiss him, or arrest him? Is it surprising that the OGPU arrests such fellows? (*Voices from the audience:* "Quite right! Absolutely right!" *Applause.*)

Lenin said that the Party can be completely wrecked if indulgence is shown to disorganisers and splitters. That is quite true. That is precisely why I think that it is high time to stop showing indulgence to the leaders of the opposition and to come to the conclusion that Trotsky and Zinoviev must be expelled from the Central Committee of our Party. (*Voices:* "Quite right!") That is the elementary conclusion and the elementary, minimum measure that must be taken in order to protect the Party from the disorganisers' splitting activities.

At the last plenum of the Central Committee and Central Control Commission, held in August this year, some members of the plenum rebuked me for being too mild with Trotsky and Zinoviev, for advising the plenum against the immediate expulsion of Trotsky and Zinoviev from the Central Committee. (*Voices from the audience:* "That's right, and we rebuke you now.") Perhaps I was too kind then and made a mistake in proposing that a milder line be adopted towards Trotsky and Zinoviev. (*Voices:* "Quite right!" *Comrade Petrovsky:* "Quite right. We shall always rebuke you for a rotten 'piece of string'!") But now, comrades, after what we have gone through during these three months, after the opposition has broken the promise to dissolve its faction that it made in its special "declaration" of August 8, thereby deceiving the Party once again, after all this, there can be no more room at all for mildness. We must now step into the front rank with those comrades who are demanding that Trotsky and Zinoviev be expelled from the Central Committee. (*Stormy applause. Voices:* "Quite right! Quite right!" *A voice from the audience:* "Trotsky should be expelled from the Party.") Let the congress decide that, comrades.

In expelling Trotsky and Zinoviev from the Central Committee, we must submit for the consideration of the Fifteenth Congress all the documents which have accumulated concerning the opposition's splitting activities, and on the basis of those documents the congress will be able to adopt an appropriate decision.

From Leninism to Trotskyism

The next question. In his speech Zinoviev touched upon the interesting question of "mistakes" in the Party's line during the past two years and of the "correctness" of the opposition's line. I should like to answer this briefly by clearing up the question of the *bankruptcy* of the opposition's line and the correctness of our Party's line during the past two years. But I am taking up too much of your attention, comrades. (*Voices:* "Please go on!" *The chairman:* "Anyone against?" *Voices:* "Please go on!")

What is the main sin of the opposition, which determined the bankruptcy of its policy? Its main sin is that it tried, is trying, and will go on trying to embellish Leninism with Trotskyism and to *replace* Leninism by Trotskyism. There was a time when Kamenev and Zinoviev defended Leninism from Trotsky's attacks. At that time Trotsky himself was not so bold. That was one line. Later, however, Zinoviev and Kamenev, frightened by new difficulties, deserted to Trotsky's side, formed something in the nature of an inferior August bloc with him and thus became captives of Trotskyism. That was further confirmation of Lenin's earlier statement that the mistake Zinoviev and Kamenev made in October was not "accidental." From fighting for Leninism, Zinoviev and Kamenev went over to the line of fighting for Trotskyism. That is an entirely different line. And that indeed explains why Trotsky has now become bolder.

What is the chief aim of the present united bloc headed by Trotsky? It is little by little to switch the Party from the Leninist course to that of Trotskyism. That is the opposition's main sin. But the Party wants to remain a Leninist party. Naturally, the Party turned its back on the opposition and raised the banner of Leninism ever higher and higher. That is why yesterday's leaders of the Party have now become renegades.

The opposition thinks that its defeat can be "explained" by the personal factor, by Stalin's rudeness, by the obstinacy of Bukharin and Rykov, and so forth. That is too cheap an explanation! It is an incantation, not an explanation. Trotsky has been fighting Leninism since 1904. From 1904 until the February Revolution in 1917 he hung around the Mensheviks, desperately fighting Lenin's Party all the time. During that period Trotsky suffered a number of defeats at the hand of Lenin's Party. Why? Perhaps Stalin's rudeness was to blame? But Stalin was not yet the secretary of the Central Committee at that time; he was not abroad, but in Russia, fighting tsarism underground, whereas the struggle between Trotsky and Lenin raged abroad. So what has Stalin's rudeness got to do with it?

During the period from the October Revolution to 1922, Trotsky, already a member of the Bolshevik Party, managed to make two "grand" sorties against Lenin and his Party: in 1918—on the question of the Brest Peace; and in 1921—on the trade-union question. Both those sorties ended in Trotsky being defeated. Why? Perhaps Stalin's rudeness was to blame here? But at that time Stalin was not yet the secretary of the Central Committee. The secretarial posts were then occupied by notorious Trotskyists. So what has Stalin's rudeness got to do with it?

Later, Trotsky made a number of fresh sorties against the Party (1923, 1924, 1926, 1927) and each sortie ended in Trotsky suffering a fresh defeat.

Is it not obvious from all this that Trotsky's fight against the Leninist Party has deep, far-reaching historical roots? Is it not obvious from this that the struggle the Party is now waging against Trotskyism is a continuation of the struggle that the Party, headed by Lenin, waged from 1904 onwards?

Is it not obvious from all this that the attempts of the Trotskyists to replace Leninism by Trotskyism are the chief cause of the failure and bankruptcy of the entire line of the opposition?

Our Party was born and grew up in the storm of revolutionary battles. It is not a party that grew up in a period of peaceful development. For that very reason it is rich in revolutionary traditions and does not make a fetish of its leaders. At one time Plekhanov was the most popular man in the Party. More than that, he was the founder of the Party, and his popularity was incomparably greater than that of Trotsky or Zinoviev. Nevertheless, in spite of that, the Party turned away from Plekhanov as soon as he began to depart from Marxism and go over to opportunism.

But the most striking indication of the opposition's opportunist degeneration, the most striking sign of the opposition's bankruptcy and fall, was its vote against the Manifesto of the Central Executive Committee of the U.S.S.R. The opposition is against the introduction of a seven-hour working day! The opposition is against the Manifesto of the Central Executive Committee of the U.S.S.R.! The entire working class of the U.S.S.R., the entire advanced section of the proletarians in all countries, enthusiastically welcome the Manifesto, unanimously applaud the idea of introducing a seven-hour working day—but the opposition votes against the Manifesto and adds its voice to the general chorus of bourgeois and Menshevik "critics," it adds its voice to those of the slanderers on the staff of *Vorwdrts*.

I did not think that the opposition could sink to such a disgrace.

Some of the Most Important Results of the Party's Policy During the Last Few Years

Let us pass now to the question of our Party's line during the past two years; let us examine and appraise it.

Zinoviev and Trotsky said that our Party's line has proved to be unsound. Let us turn to the facts. Let us take four principal questions of our policy and examine our Party's line during the past two years from the standpoint of these questions. I have in mind such decisive questions as that of the peasantry, that of industry and its re-equipment, that of peace, and, lastly, that of the growth of the communist elements throughout the world.

The question of the peasantry. What was the situation in our country two or three years ago? You know that the situation in the countryside was a serious one. Our Volost Executive Committee chairmen, and officials in the countryside generally, were not always recognised and were often the victims of terrorism. Village correspondents were met with sawn-off rifles. Here and there, especially in the border regions, there were bandit activities; and in a country like Georgia there were even revolts. Naturally, in such a situation the kulaks gained strength, the middle peasants rallied round the kulaks, and the poor peasants became disunited. The situation in the country was aggravated particularly by the fact that the productive forces in the countryside grew very slowly, part of the arable land remained quite untilled, and the crop area was about 70 to 75 per cent of the prewar area. This was in the period before the Fourteenth Conference of our Party.

At the Fourteenth Conference the Party adopted a number of measures in the shape of certain concessions to the middle peasants designed to accelerate the progress of peasant economy, increase the output of agricultural produce—food and raw materials, establish a stable alliance with the middle peasants, and hasten the isolation of the kulaks. At the Fourteenth Congress of our Party, the opposition, headed by Zinoviev and Kamenev, tried to disrupt this policy of the Party and proposed that we adopt instead what was, in essence, the policy of de-kulakisation, a policy of restoring the Poor Peasants' Committees. In essence, that was a policy of reverting to civil war in the countryside. The Party repulsed this attack of the opposition; it endorsed the decisions of the Fourteenth Conference, approved the policy of revitalising the Soviets in the countryside and advanced the slogan of industrialisation as the main slogan of socialist construction. The Party steadfastly kept to the line of establishing a stable alliance with the middle peasants and of isolating the kulaks.

What did the Party achieve by this?

What it achieved was that peace was established in the countryside, relations with the main mass of the peasantry were improved, conditions were created for organising the poor peasants into an independent political force, the kulaks were still further isolated and the state and co-operative bodies gradually extended their activities to the individual farms of millions of peasants.

What does peace in the countryside mean? It is one of the fundamental conditions for the building of socialism. We cannot build socialism if we have bandit activities and peasant revolts. The crop area has now been brought up to pre-war dimensions (95 per cent), we have peace in the countryside, an alliance with the middle peasants, a more or less organised poor peasantry, strengthened rural Soviets and the enhanced prestige of the proletariat and its Party in the countryside.

We have thus created the conditions that enable us to push forward the offensive against the capitalist elements in the countryside and to ensure further success in the building of socialism in our country.

Such are the results of our Party's policy in the countryside during the two years.

Thus, it follows that our Party's policy on the major question o the relations between the proletariat and the peasantry has proved to be correct.

The question of industry. History tells us that so far not a single young state in the world has developed its industry, and its heavy industry in particular, without outside assistance, without foreign loans or without plundering other countries, colonies, and so forth. That is the ordinary path of capitalist industrialisation. Britain developed her industry in the past by draining the vital sap from all countries, from all colonies, for hundreds of years and investing the loot in her industry. Germany has begun to rise lately because she has received loans from America amounting to several thousand million rubles.

We, however, cannot proceed by any of these paths. Colonial plunder is precluded by our entire policy. And we are not granted loans. Only one path is left to us, the path indicated by Lenin, namely: to raise our industry, to re-equip our industry on the basis of internal accumulations. The opposition has been croaking all the time about internal accumulations not being sufficient for the re-equipment of our industry. As far back as April 1926, the opposition asserted at a plenum of the Central Committee that our internal accumulations would not suffice for making headway with the re-equipment of our industry. At that time the opposition predicted that we would suffer failure after failure. Nevertheless, on making a check it has turned out that we have succeeded in making headway with the re-equipment of our industry during these two years. It is a fact that during the two years we have managed to invest over two thousand million rubles in our industry. It is a fact that these investments have proved to be sufficient to make further headway with the re-equipment of our industry and the industrialisation of the country. We have achieved what no other state in the world has yet achieved: we have raised our industry, we have begun to re-equip it, we have made headway in this matter on the basis of our own accumulations.

There you have the results of our policy on the question of the re-equipment of our industry.

Only the blind can deny the fact that our Party's policy in this matter has proved to be correct.

The question of foreign policy. The aim of our foreign policy, if one has in mind diplomatic relations with bourgeois states, is to maintain peace. What have we achieved in this sphere? What we have achieved is that we have upheld—well or ill, nevertheless we have upheld— *peace.* What we have achieved is that, in spite of the capitalist encirclement, in spite of the hostile activities of the capitalist governments, in spite of the provocative sorties in Peking, London and Paris — in spite of all this, we have not allowed ourselves to be provoked and have succeeded in defending the cause of peace.

We are not at war in spite of the repeated prophecies of Zinoviev and others—that is the fundamental fact in face of which all the hysterics of our opposition are of no avail. And this is important for us, because only under peace conditions can we promote the building of socialism in our country at the rate that we desire. Yet how many prophecies of war there have been! Zi-noviev prophesied that we should be at war in the spring of this year. Later he prophesied that in all probability war would break out in the autumn of this year. Nevertheless, we are already facing the winter, but still there is no war.

Such are the results of our peace policy.

Only the blind can fail to see these results.

Lastly, the fourth question—that of the state of the communist forces throughout the world. Only the blind can deny that the Communist Parties are growing throughout the world, from China to America, from Britain to Germany. Only the blind can deny that the elements of the crisis of capitalism are growing and not diminishing. Only the blind can deny that the progress in the building of socialism in our country, the successes of our policy within the country, are one of the chief reasons for the growth of the communist movement throughout the world. Only the blind can deny the progressive increase in influence and prestige of the Communist International in all countries of the world.

Such are the results of our Party's line on the four principal questions of home and foreign policy during the past two years.

What does the correctness of our Party's policy signify? Apart from everything else, it can signify only one thing: the utter bankruptcy of the policy of our opposition.

Back to Axelrod

That is all very well, we may be told. The opposition's line is wrong, it is an anti-Party line. Its tactics cannot be called anything else than splitting tactics. The expulsion of Zinoviev and Trotsky is therefore the natural way out of the situation that has arisen. All that is true.

But there was a time when we all said that the leaders of the opposition must be kept in the Central Committee, that they should not be expelled. Why this change now? How is this turn to be explained? And is there a turn at all?

Yes, there is. How is it to be explained? It is due to the radical change that has taken place in the fundamental policy and organisational "scheme" of the leaders of the opposition. The leaders of the opposition, and primarily Trotsky, have changed for the worse. Naturally, this was bound to cause a change in the Party's policy towards these oppositionists.

Let us take, for example, such an important question of principle as that of the degeneration of our Party. What is meant by the degeneration of our Party? Itmeans denying the existence of the dictatorship of the proletariat in the U.S.S.R. What was Trotsky's position in this matter, say, about three years ago? You know that at that time the liberals and Mensheviks, the Smena-Vekhists and all kinds of renegades kept on reiterating that the degeneration of our Party was inevitable. You know that at that time they quoted examples from the French revolution and asserted that the Bolsheviks were bound to suffer the same collapse as the Jacobins in their day suffered in France. You know that historical analogies with the French revolution (the downfall of the Jacobins) were then and are today the chief argument advanced by all the various Mensheviks and Smena-Vekhists against the maintenance of the proletarian dictatorship and the possibility of building socialism in our country.

What was Trotsky's attitude towards this three years ago? He was certainly opposed to the drawing of such analogies. Here is what he wrote at that time in his pamphlet *The New Course* (1924):

"The historical analogies with the Great French Revolution (the downfall of the Jacobins!) which liberalism and Menshevism utilise and console themselves with *are superficial and unsound"* (see *The New Course,* p. 33)

Clear and definite! It would be difficult, I think, to express oneself more emphatically and definitely. Was Trotsky right in what he then said about the historical analogies with the French revolution that were being zealously advanced by all sorts of Smena-Vekhists and Mensheviks? Absolutely right.

But now? Does Trotsky still adopt that position? Unfortunately, he does not. On the contrary even. During these three years Trotsky has managed to evolve in the direction of "Menshevism" and "liberalism." Now he himself asserts that drawing historical analogies with the French revolution is a sign not of Menshevism, but of "real," "genuine" "Leninism." Have you read the verbatim report of the meeting of the Presidium of the Central Control Commission held in July this year? If you have, you will easily understand that in his struggle against the Party Trotsky is now basing himself on the Menshevik theories about the degeneration of our Party on the lines of the downfall of the Jacobins in the period of the French revolution. Today, Trotsky thinks that twaddle about "Thermidor" is a sign of good taste.

From Trotskyism to "Menshevism" and "liberalism" in the fundamental question of degeneration—such is the path that the Trotskyists have travelled during the past three years.

The Trotskyists have changed. The Party's policy towards the Trotskyists has also had to change.

Let us now take a no less important question, such as that of organisation, of Party discipline, of the submission of the minority to the majority, of the role played by iron Party discipline in strengthening the dictatorship of the proletariat. Everybody knows that iron discipline in our Party is one of the fundamental conditions for maintaining the dictatorship of the proletariat and for success in building socialism in our country. Everybody knows that the first thing the Mensheviks in all countries try to do is to undermine the iron discipline in our Party. There was a time when Trotsky understood and appreciated the importance of iron discipline in our Party. Properly speaking, the disagreements between our Party and Trotsky never ceased, but Trotsky and the Trotskyists were clever enough to submit to the decisions of our Party. Everybody is aware of Trotsky's repeated statement that, no matter what our Party might be, he was ready to "stand to attention" whenever the Party ordered. And it must be said that often the Trotskyists succeeded in remaining loyal to the Party and to its leading bodies.

But now? Can it be said that the Trotskyists, the present opposition, are ready to submit to the Party's decisions, to stand to attention, and so forth? No. That cannot be said any longer. After they have twice broken their promise to submit to the Party's decisions, after they have twice deceived the Party, after they have organised illegal printing presses in conjunction with bourgeois intellectuals, after the repeated statements of Zinoviev and Trotsky made from this very rostrum that they were violating the discipline of our Party and would continue to do so—after all that it is doubtful whether a single person will be found in our Party who would dare to believe that the leaders of the opposition are ready to stand to attention before the Party. The opposition has now shifted to a new line, the line of splitting the Party, the line of creating a new party. The most popular pamphlet among the oppositionists at the present time is not Lenin's Bolshevik pamphlet *One Step Forward, Two Steps Back,* but Trotsky's old Menshevik pamphlet *Our Political Task* (published in 1904), written in opposition to the organisational principles of Leninism, in opposition to Lenin's pamphlet *One Step Forward, Two Steps Back.*

You know that the essence of that old pamphlet of Trotsky's is repudiation of the Leninist conception of the Party and of Party discipline. In that pamphlet Trotsky never calls Lenin anything but "Maximilien Lenin," hinting that Lenin was another Maximilien Robespierre, striving, like the latter, for personal dictatorship. In that pamphlet Trotsky plainly says that Party discipline need be submitted to only to the degree that Party decisions do not contradict the wishes and views of those who are called upon to submit to the Party. That is a purely Menshevik principle of organisation. Incidentally that pamphlet is interesting because Trotsky dedicates it to the Menshevik P. Axelrod. That is what he says: "To my dear teacher Pavel Borisovich Axelrod." (*Laughter. Voices:* "An out-and-out Menshevik!")

From loyalty to the Party to the policy of splitting the Party, from Lenin's pamphlet *One Step Forward, Two Steps Back* to Trotsky's pamphlet *Our Political Tasks,* from Lenin to Axelrod — such is the organisational path that our opposition has travelled.

The Trotskyists have changed. The Party's organisational policy towards the Trotskyist opposition has also had to change.

Well, a good riddance! Go to your "dear teacher Pavel Borisovich Axelrod"! A good riddance! Only make haste, most worthy Trotsky, for, in view of his senility, "Pavel Borisovich" may die soon, and you may not reach your "teacher" in time. *(Prolonged applause.)*

9 781716 016639